BLONDIN: HERO OF NIAGARA

BLONDIN: HERO OF NIAGARA

Richard A. Boning

Illustrated by Jim Sharpe

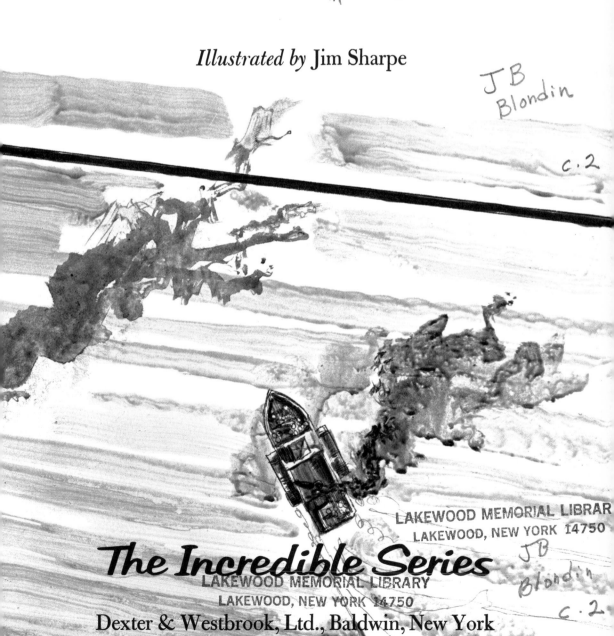

The Incredible Series

Dexter & Westbrook, Ltd., Baldwin, New York

Printed in the United States of America

International Standard Book Number: 0-87966-101-1

To
Coleman Morrison

Gamblers at the Cataract House were joyful at last. They had found few victims during that year of 1859. In fact, some had thought of returning to the greener fields of New York City in spite of charges of murder and theft awaiting them there. But they had just heard exciting news — news that spelled profit — even riches to them. Some mad French acrobat had announced that he would walk across the gorge at Niagara Falls on a tightrope — a feat everyone knew to be impossible!

"We'll bet everything we have that he doesn't make it," a gambler in a tall beaver hat whispered to the others. "Then — if necessary — we'll *see* to it that he doesn't. We'll clean up!" Their eyes gleamed greedily.

The cliffs on both the American and Canadian sides of the Falls were 200 feet high — higher than a twenty-story building. Who would suspect anything but an accident?

The plotters were still chuckling when a slim, blond man entered the lobby. "I am Blondin," he announced to the desk clerk. "This is my manager, Mr. Harry Colcord. Would someone guide us to the highest cliffs?"

Winking at the others, the gambler in the beaver hat spoke up. "We'd be happy to," he sneered. Nudging one another, the gamblers arose and accompanied the slender Frenchman and his manager to the cliffs. The sight was awe-inspiring. Tall pine trees far below looked like toys. In the distance loomed the rugged cliffs of the Canadian side. "Of course you aren't serious about this plan of yours, are you?" The gambler studied Blondin with cold eyes.

"Absolutely serious," replied the acrobat. "Why do you doubt it?"

"You'll have no objection, then, if my friends and I wager rather large amounts that you will not succeed?"

"None whatsoever," the confident Blondin replied.

Colcord turned pale at this, and a look of doubt crossed his face. He knew that he and Blondin could make a fortune from such a crossing, but he didn't like the looks of those cardplayers! He glanced anxiously at Blondin. "The wind is strong too," he murmured. "Very strong!" Instinct told him that these men would attempt to kill his friend before allowing him to succeed. "Give it up — they mean to kill you," he whispered. "It's too much of a risk."

Blondin paid no heed. "Wager what you choose," he told the gamblers. "No one has ever attempted a crossing like this before. I will be the first — on June 30th. Thank you for your courtesy, messieurs. I invite you to be my guests."

At the Cataract House Harry overheard one of the gamblers — "Thank you for your courtesy, messieurs —." The mockery was greeted with laughter. Colcord shuddered.

None of this disturbed Blondin. After all, he had made his career and his reputation by astounding audiences with death-defying acts.

Born Jean Francois Gravelet in Hesdin, France, he had first amazed his own neighbors by swinging through the treetops at the age of five.

At six he had strung a rope between two gateposts and walked across, balancing himself with an oar. His parents had sent him to the special school for acrobats at Lyons, and at ten he was billed as "The Little Wonder."

Colcord knew all this, and knew too that Blondin was the greatest of all acrobats — but his misgivings persisted.

A local merchant donated the 1500-foot rope, one end of which was secured to rocks on the Canadian side. The other was made fast on the American side. Colcord's eyes bulged. "Look!" he gasped. The rope was sagging and swaying alarmingly. Guy ropes were added, but still the rope swayed dangerously with each gust of wind.

The gamblers smiled contentedly as they saw this, and the odds against Blondin rose higher.

At three o'clock on the afternoon of June 30th, both sides of the gorge were jammed with spectators. Many had paid as much as fifty cents for choice locations. They would have an excellent view of the Frenchman's death plunge!

An hour later a carriage swept up on the American side of the Falls. Blondin, dressed in spangled cape and tights, stepped out and bowed to the crowd. The people stared at him curiously — many considered him already a dead man. Colcord's face was chalky. "Be careful — very careful," he pleaded.

Blondin smiled, picked up the thirty-eight-foot balancing pole, and stepped lightly onto the rope. The guy ropes made it appear that the Frenchman was balanced on one strand of a gigantic spider web. He was only a speck to the people below, and the rope, if visible at all, a mere thread.

Watching tensely, the crowd fell silent as Blondin inched his way out over the gorge. At the midpoint he placed his feet with care and, timing his sway with that of the rope, he stopped, sank to his knees — and lay on the rope as if on a swaying hammock! The crowds gasped. Rocked by the wind, he appeared to be asleep — as the water churned far below.

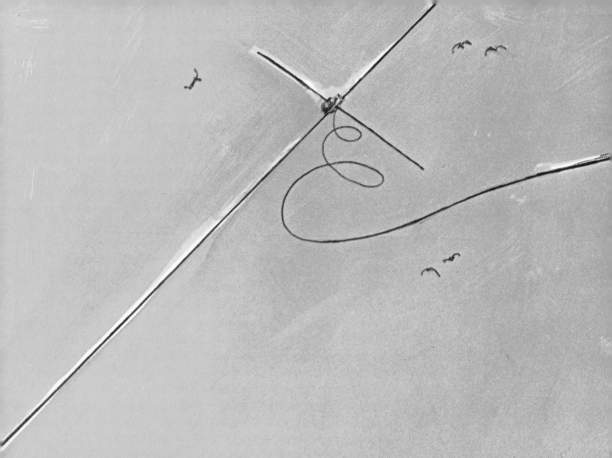

Harry's knuckles turned white as his fists clenched in fear, but the amazing Frenchman rose slowly, stretched like a man refreshed from sleep, and proceeded to lower a long cord. A small ship, the *Maid of the Mist*, appeared below. A hand reached for the cord and attached a small flask. Pulling it up, hand over hand, Blondin drank — bowed in thanks — and casually tossed the empty flask to the waters below.

In exactly eighteen minutes he was in Canada. Wild
cheers rose on both sides. He began his return. As
Colcord watched anxiously, he saw something that sent
a chill down his spine.

Faced with enormous losses, the gamblers rushed to
the guy ropes and began shaking them violently. The
main rope lashed and coiled like a giant serpent. The
crowd gazed in horror.

Harry fought his way into the mass of people, trying to reach the gamblers, but it was no use. Blondin wavered. It seemed impossible that he could regain his balance. Moving his pole rapidly as the whiplike motions of the rope threatened to hurl him into space, he suddenly sprinted ahead and in moments was safely on the American side.

23

That night at the Cataract House, Harry was still limp from the day's events. Blondin, however, bubbled with energy and confidence. As they entered the dining room, he patted his wallet. "A good day for us, eh, Harry?" Harry was speechless. He saw the gamblers hunched over their cards, whispering together — and he knew they would try again.

For two summers Blondin capered on the tightrope as Harry watched fearfully. Each new stunt was more daring — and more dangerous — than the last. Police now guarded the guy ropes, but the gamblers continued to bet against the Frenchman. They lost — and lost — and lost!

Once Blondin actually carried a twenty-pound stove out on the rope, proceeded to cook an omelet — and calmly washed it down with a glass of wine!

27

Another feat involved a backward somersault as the rope swayed alarmingly. Thousands turned away, unable to face what seemed certain suicide, but the gamblers watched eagerly.

This amazing man even strolled the rope at night in the white glare of a locomotive's headlight! Blondin could see the rope stretching out into the blackness and swaying in the cool night breeze. He carefully edged ahead.

Crack! The sound of a rifle was heard, and the bright beam of light disappeared. Blondin vanished from sight — only to reappear moments later on the other side.

Blondin continued his performances. He made the trip blindfolded to prove that his crossing in the dark was not mere luck. He stood on a chair, which he balanced carefully on the rope.

By now, all his friends pleaded with him to stop. "We have plenty of money," urged Harry. "Let's call it quits. Why tempt fate?"

But Blondin had a new idea. "Harry, see to it that all the reporters are in the lobby tonight. I shall make an announcement which I think will prove interesting."

That evening the acrobat spoke directly to the gamblers, who eyed him suspiciously. "Messieurs," he said, "I know that all of you have followed my every action with *great* interest. I now announce a new undertaking." He paused dramatically. "I shall next cross carrying someone on my back — a volunteer."

The gamblers gasped in surprise, as the reporters noted every word. Crossing the gorge alone was one thing — but to carry another would mean certain death for both. "Who is your volunteer?" snarled a gambler.

Blondin shrugged. "I do not know as yet. Perhaps one of you —?" The gamblers suddenly became interested in other matters! The acrobat smiled and nodded.

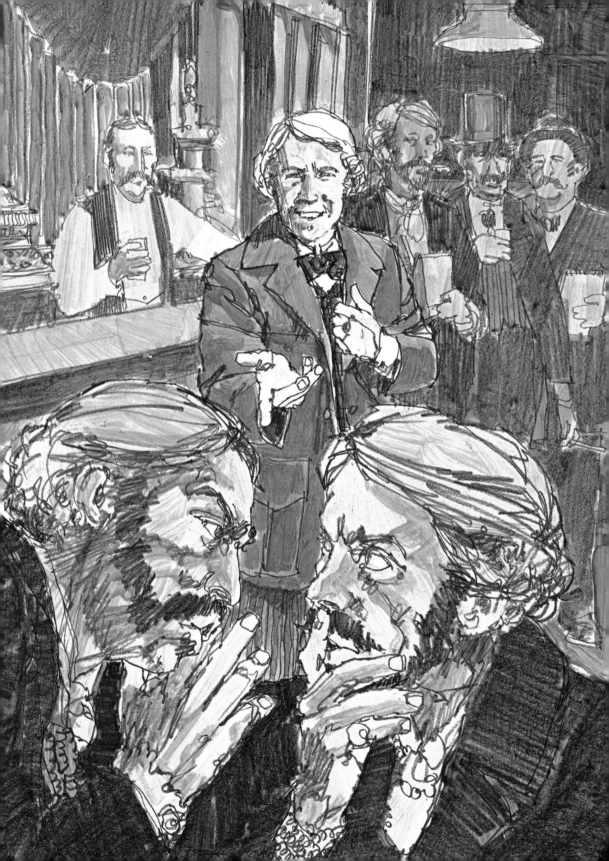

Days were spent seeking the volunteer. It seemed that the idea must be abandoned. Then Harry, pale and tense, approached Blondin. "I will be your volunteer," he said simply.

Blondin could not believe his ears. At first he was inclined to laugh, but the expression on Harry's face sobered him. "Thank you, Harry," he said seriously. "It will not be as difficult as they think. Just remember a few simple instructions. On the rope you must take everything slowly — very slowly. If I should sway or falter, remain perfectly still and do not try to help me."

"Sway or f-f-falter?" stammered Harry.

Blondin shrugged. "It is always possible. Just remember not to move. Above all, never look down."

Colcord nodded numbly.

The day arrived all too swiftly for Harry. Special trains arrived, and Blondin estimated the size of the crowd to be at least 300,000. It was a record — one that could well stand for all time. Dressed in formal evening clothes for the occasion, Harry seemed unconcerned about the size of the crowd.

He mounted to Blondin's back with the aid of a pair of special stirrups attached to the acrobat. Blondin moved forward slowly.

37

As they progressed, Harry suddenly realized that his friend was perspiring heavily. The extra weight was having its effect! He also saw the gamblers grinning in anticipation. Despite Blondin's instructions, he glanced downward — and quickly raised his eyes!

They were nearing the midpoint — when Blondin stumbled! To regain his balance he began to move faster. Tottering, he reached a guy rope. It parted with a loud snap! The gamblers had been at work again!

His chest heaving, Blondin plunged ahead to the next guy rope, where he paused. "Harry," he gasped, "get off for a moment while I rest."

Slowly, as if in a dream, Colcord did so. After what seemed hours, he felt the swaying rope beneath his feet. Horrified, he clutched the acrobat around the hips. He remembered Blondin's warning, but his eyes were drawn to the waters below. A feeling of dizziness swept over him.

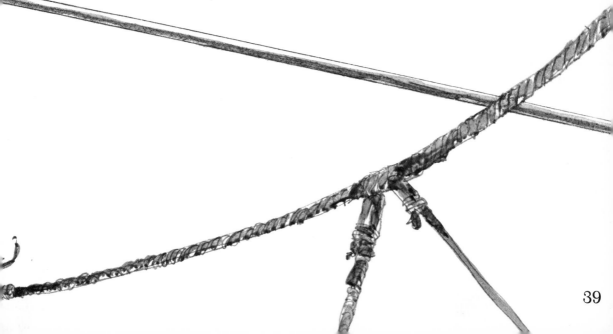

"Harry!" Blondin spoke sharply. "Climb back up again!" Shaking with fear, Harry somehow managed to place his feet in the stirrups and mount once more.

Seven times Blondin ordered Colcord off his back. Each time the manager trembled behind his friend, with nothing between himself and death but the swaying rope. Each time he remounted.

As the two neared the American side, the gamblers, enraged at facing certain ruin, broke through the police line and began to shake the rope wildly. Blondin's eyes blazed with anger and determination. He sprinted for safety — then staggered the last few yards. The roar of the crowd echoed along the cliffs.

Harry Colcord eventually left the world of the tight-rope and became a portrait painter. Years later, after having relived the experience many times, Colcord revealed details. "The memory still haunts me. I see the cliffs, black with people — the waters far below — Blondin stumbling, the rope swaying, the wild dash for life. I live the horror over and over again."

As for Blondin himself, he returned to Europe and became the chief attraction at London's Crystal Palace. For thirty-seven years he continued his thrilling feats. At an age when some men have difficulty getting out of bed, he was crossing a tightrope on stilts!

At the age of seventy-two, Blondin retired from the rope. The following year he became ill. As he lay in bed surrounded by his loved ones, the sounds of Niagara returned. Once more he was at the Falls — crossing the gorge. A long rope stretched before him — longer than any he had ever seen. "No, Harry," Blondin whispered. "I can't take you with me. This time I'll cross alone."

Blondin crossed — into eternity and everlasting fame.

47